P9-DOA-670

Discovering

ANTS

Christopher O'Toole

Illustrations by Wendy Meadway

The Bookwright Press
New York · 1986

Discovering Nature

Discovering Ants
Discovering Bees and Wasps
Discovering Birds of Prey
Discovering Butterflies and Moths
Discovering Frogs and Toads

Discovering Rabbits and Hares
Discovering Snakes and Lizards
Discovering Spiders
Discovering Worms

Further titles are in preparation

All photographs from Oxford Scientific Films

First published in the
United States in 1986 by
The Bookwright Press
387 Park Avenue South
New York, NY 10016

First published in 1986 by
Wayland (Publishers) Limited
61 Western Road, Hove
East Sussex, BN3 1JD, England

© Copyright 1986 Wayland (Publishers) Limited

ISBN 0-531-18056-5
Library of Congress Catalog Card Number: 85-73663

Typeset by Alphabet Limited
Printed in Italy by Sagdos S.p.A., Milan

Cover *A red ant taking pollen from a figwort flower.*

Frontispiece *A carton ant from Trinidad displays its sharp jaws.*

Contents

1
Introducing Ants

A group of ants chewing up a cockroach.

What are Ants?

Ants are insects: they are actually a special group of wasps. There are about 10,000 different kinds of ants in the world. They are found in almost every country except in the very cold areas.

All ants are **social** and live in **colonies**. Each colony contains at least one egg-laying female called the **queen** and several thousands or even millions of workers. Workers are females too, but they do not lay eggs. Instead, they spend their lives gathering food, building the nest and looking after the queen and her young. Workers are the wingless ants we see in our gardens. Male ants have wings and they are usually only seen during the time of year when **mating** takes place.

Ants nest in lots of different places: in the soil, under stones or in dead wood. Some use hollow plant stems and some even weave living leaves together to make a nest.

Ants eat many different kinds of food, such as insects, dead animals, seeds and nectar. Some very special kinds of ant eat a fungus which they grow in underground gardens.

Ants that nest in the ground bring many plants and animals as food into their nests, which enriches the soil. This makes ants very important.

A wood ant drags a dead fly back to the nest.

The Ant's Body

Most of the ants we see are the wingless workers. The ant, like all insects, has a body enclosed in an outer skeleton and divided into three parts: the head, the **thorax** and the **abdomen**. The head contains the brain, the eyes, the jaws, and the feelers, or **antennae**. The thorax is muscular and bears three pairs of legs as well as the wings of males and queens. The abdomen is the hind part of the body and contains the stomach and glands that make special scents and poisons. In queens the abdomen contains the **ovaries**, which make eggs, and in males it contains the **testes**, which make **sperm**.

The waist between the thorax and

You can clearly see this red ant's antennae and an eye on either side of its head.

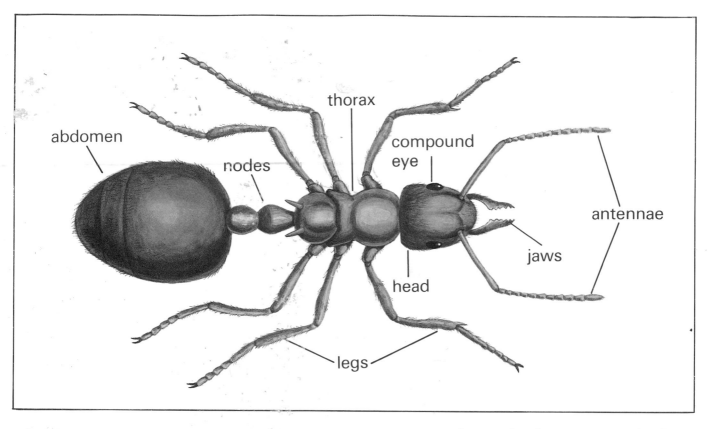

abdomen

thorax

nodes

compound
eye

antennae

jaws

head

legs

The body of an ant with each part labeled.

the abdomen has either one or two bumps called **nodes**. The black garden ant has one node, while the red garden ant has two nodes.

Ants go through three stages before becoming adults – egg, **larva** and **pupa**. In the pupal stage, the inside of the larva's body is broken down and reformed into the adult. This is the same as the chrysalis or cocoon stage in butterflies and moths.

Starting a Colony

On hot summer days, you may have noticed large swarms of flying ants. These are the mating flights that must take place before new colonies can be started.

The newly-emerged winged males and queens fly high into the air and mate. The males may mate several times with different queens. They die after a few days. After she has mated, usually only once, the queen returns to the ground and sheds her wings. Now she looks for a place to begin a

A queen army ant with a much smaller worker ant on her back.

nest. This may be a dead tree stump, a hollow twig or in the ground.

Black ant queens prepare to fly.

The queen seals herself inside a little chamber or cell and an amazing thing happens; the wing muscles and fat in her thorax break down and are used to make eggs in her ovaries. She loses about half her body weight and soon starts to lay lots of eggs, some of which hatch into larvae. The larvae become workers, and all the time the queen keeps on laying eggs, some of which are eaten by the workers and larvae, until there are enough workers to gather food for the whole colony. In a cold climate the queen and her **brood** remain in the nest all winter and stop all activities until the spring.

This is the way most ant colonies are started. Sometimes, several queens may start a colony together. Colonies may last for many years.

The Life of a Worker

Worker ants do all the "household" duties. They keep the nest clean, repair any damage and build new sections to house the growing colony.

Another important job is the care of eggs and larvae. Workers on nursery duty lick the eggs and larvae frequently to keep them free from mold and tiny insects called mites. The larvae are fed on liquid food from the mouths of workers.

Workers have jobs to do outside the nest, too. They visit flowers for nectar. They also gather **honeydew** from aphids. Some are **scavengers** and others kill for food. Some special kinds of ants, called harvester ants, collect and store seeds.

You will usually find a lot of ants at

Army ant soldiers and workers with their prey, a grasshopper.

Above *An ant with nectar in its jaws.*

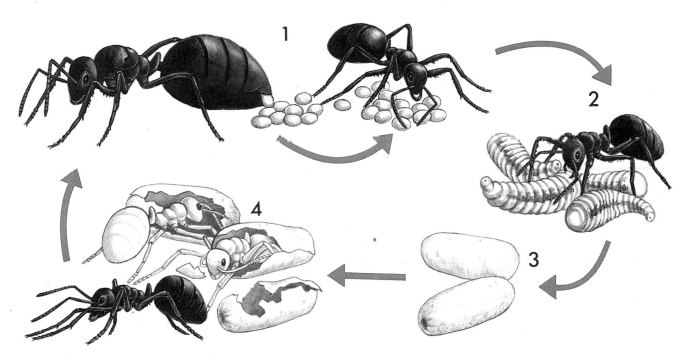

The life cycle of an ant: 1. queen lays eggs; 2. workers tend larvae; 3. pupae; 4. adults emerge from pupae and gradually harden and darken.

a source of food. This is because a worker can direct other workers from the nest to the food she has found. There are three ways of doing this. A large worker may simply carry a smaller one to the food. Some species use tandem running; a returned worker tugs the antennae of another ant, which follows her, keeping in constant touch with her antennae,

until they reach the food. Other kinds, like the red and black garden ants, lay a trail of scent from the food source to the nest. The workers quickly follow it and find the food.

2
The Nest

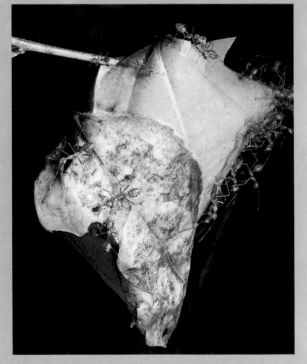

These Australian tree ants weave leaves together to make a nest.

Nests in Trees

A nest is a safe place where the ant colony can live and rear its young. Wherever a nest is, it must give the ants some protection from enemies and bad weather.

All over the world, trees provide ants with places to live. Many ants nest in crevices in rough bark. Others use beetle borings in dead branches. One ant, found in Britain and Europe, uses dead tree stumps. This is the shiny black ant, a relative of the black garden ant. It digs out galleries in the wood, lining them with carton, a mixture of finely chewed wood, honeydew and **saliva**. As the colony gets older, more and more of the wood is replaced with carton.

The weaver ants are some of the most interesting tree-living ants. They live in warm, tropical countries and are found in Africa, Asia and northern Australia. They are called weaver ants because they weave together living leaves to make a nest. They do this in an unusual way.

Large workers draw suitable leaves together by holding on to one leaf with their jaws and digging their claws into another. Smaller workers, each with a larva clasped in its jaws, weave the leaves together with side-to-side movements of their heads, using silk squirted out by the larvae. Damage to the nest can be repaired in the same way.

Wood-boring ants nest in trees. They chew their way through the wood, making networks of tunnels.

Mound Nests

Wild countryside, with well-drained soil which has never been plowed, is the home of the yellow meadow ant. This ant, like the black garden ant, often starts to build a nest under a stone. But, in time, it builds up a mound of soil which eventually surrounds and covers the original stone. The soil that forms the mound is dug from as deep as 1 m (3 ft) below the ground.

The colony lives partly inside the mound and partly underground. Because it is raised above the ground by as much as 40 to 60 cm (15 to 23 in), the mound catches the sun and soon warms up. The soil in the mound may be 7°C (12.5°F) warmer than the surrounding soil. Of course, it will cool down quickly in a cold wind, but the ants simply move themselves and their brood down

A mound nest made of soil bound by plant roots.

into the underground part of the nest.

Yellow meadow ants are rarely seen outside the nest because they feed on soil insects and small worms. They also eat honeydew made by tiny, root-feeding **aphids**.

Rabbits like to sit on ant mounds. Their droppings and urine fertilize the soil and encourage plants to grow on top of the mound. The ants fill the tunnels in the mound with their own

Wood ants make mound nests from small pieces of wood.

droppings. This encourages the growth of roots belonging to these plants. The roots bind the soil of the mound and keep it solid. They also provide food for the aphids. Yellow ant mounds are therefore an important part of a whole community of living things.

In the Ground

Many kinds of ants nest in the soil. Often, the nest is dug underneath a flat stone or a log. Under paving stones in gardens are favorite places, especially for the black garden ant. Workers of this ant often come indoors to find sugar and crumbs.

The nest of the black garden ant is 2 to 5 cm (1 to 2 in) deep and consists of lots of chambers or cells joined by interlocking tunnels. Sometimes there are so many tunnels that the nest looks like a sponge. The chambers are used to keep eggs and larvae in separate groups. The larvae themselves are kept in groups according to age.

Nursery workers also move the young around the nest so that they

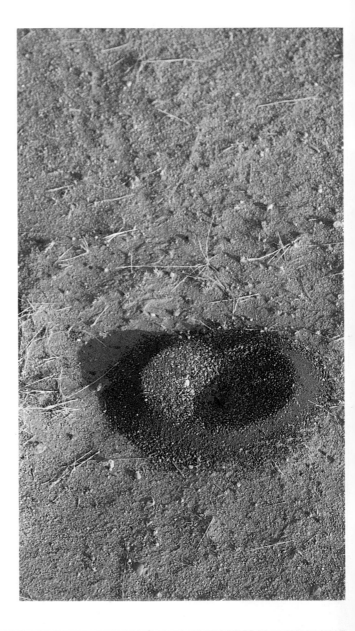

An ant nest in the Sahara Desert.

can enjoy the best temperatures for growth. You can test this yourself. Look under a flat stone covering an ant nest. If it is a warm day, but not too hot, you will see the eggs and larvae all in their separate groups just under the stone. Take a look later in the evening, when it is cooler. The nest will appear deserted, because the workers will have taken the young into deeper and warmer chambers in the soil.

If you could look into an ant nest under the ground this is what you might see.

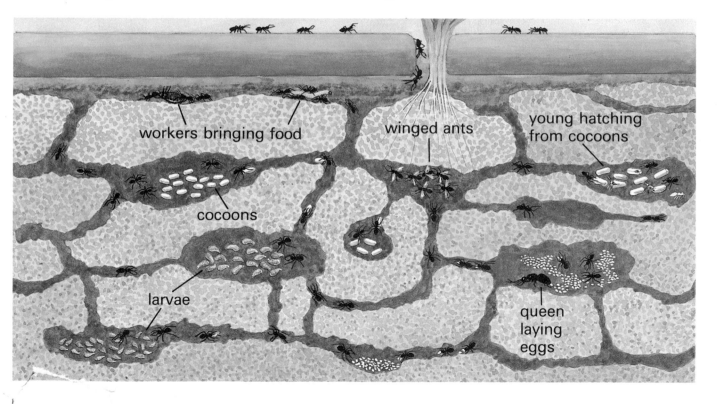

workers bringing food

winged ants

young hatching from cocoons

cocoons

larvae

queen laying eggs

3
Special Ants

The jaws of a bulldog ant.

Bulldog Ants

Bulldog ants live only in Australia. The workers are among the largest of all ants, being 1 to 3½ cm (½ to 1½ in) long. They are reddish brown and run rapidly over the ground. People in Australia try to avoid them because they have a very nasty sting. They are called bulldog ants because of their very large jaws, each equipped with many teeth.

The underground nest of bulldog ants is made up of large chambers connected by vertical tunnels and is from 1 to 2 m (3 to 6½ ft) deep. Bulldog ants have colonies with between a few hundred to just over a thousand workers. The workers forage singly, hunting insect **prey** and stinging it to death. They take the prey back to the nest, cut it up into pieces and feed them to the larvae. Large workers do most of the hunting.

Smaller ones take prey from the larger ones and give it to the larvae.

The queen scatters her round eggs singly over the floors of the chambers. Unlike the queens of most other ants, the bulldog queen does not start a colony by sealing herself up in a chamber, using her wing muscles and fat to produce eggs. Instead, she leaves the nest regularly to hunt for prey until the first workers hatch out. Only then does she shed her wings.

A worker bulldog ant searches for food on the forest floor.

Army and Driver Ants

Army ants live in the forests of South America. They have no permanent nest because they are on the move most of the time, in massive, marching columns, carrying their young with them. At night they have a temporary resting place in a rock crevice or hollow tree. Sometimes, they stay for up to three weeks in one place, but usually they move on each morning.

A colony may have between 15,000 and 700,000 members. It swarms out in raids to hunt prey, which is mostly other insects and small creatures living in the **leaf litter**. The raiding

A column of army ants in Trinidad.

column can be 105 m (344 ft) long and 8 m (26 ft) wide, and spreads out like a fan.

The workers are all blind, and raiding swarms follow scent trails laid by scout workers. Some workers are very large, with massive, curved jaws. These ants are called soldiers. They stand on either side of the column, facing outward, guarding the hunting workers.

In Africa, driver ants live much the same kind of life. However, they stay longer in their resting places than the army ants and often dig deep into the soil. Their raiding columns can catch and kill prey as large as lizards and snakes.

A temporary nest made by army ants.

Leaf-cutter Ants

In the wet forests of tropical South America, leaf-cutter ants are everywhere. They can be seen marching back to their underground nests, each clasping a fresh piece of cut, green leaf in its jaws. Leaf-cutters are the main destroyers of leaves in South America. But the leaves are not used for food. Instead, the millions of workers in a colony use the leaves as a **compost** for growing a special kind of fungus. In other words, the ants are gardeners and the fungus that they grow is their food.

The ants cultivate the fungus by giving it a mixture of insect droppings

Leaf-cutter ants cutting leaves.

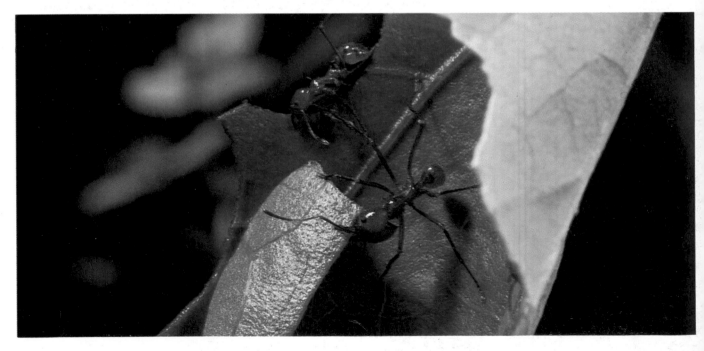

A leaf-cutter queen in her fungus garden.

and finely chewed leaves on which to grow. The droppings are mainly from grasshoppers and beetles and they can be found all over the forest floor.

The fungus that the ants grow is found nowhere else but in their nests. The ants weed out all other fungi except the one they like to eat. This fungus forms a dense, spongy mass of fine white threads. The threads have swollen tips which contain the food the ants need. The ants create the perfect growing conditions for the fungus and the fungus provides the ants with food. This kind of relationship between two or more different types of organisms living together is called **symbiosis**.

4
Ants and Other Living Things

Black ants "milking" aphids.

Ants and Aphids

Ants have a very special symbiotic relationship with insects called aphids. These are soft-bodied bugs, also known as plant lice, which drink the sap of plants. The aphids produce partially digested sap from their rear ends. This is a sweet mixture of sugars called honeydew, which ants love.

If you look carefully at the plants in the garden, you may find some black aphids being visited by ants. Look carefully, and you will see the ants stroke the aphids with their antennae. This makes the aphids produce honeydew, which the ants lap up and store in their **crops**. Later, they will take it back to their nest and feed it to the queen and larvae. Sometimes, you will see an ant pass some honeydew, mouth-to-mouth, to another worker.

The ants that attend aphids really do look after them. They chase away enemies, such as flowerfly grubs and ladybugs, which would otherwise eat the aphids. In return, the aphids allow the ants to "milk" them for honeydew.

Even ants that spend all their lives underground, such as the yellow meadow ant, enjoy honeydew. They extend their nest burrows to areas containing plant roots with root-feeding aphids.

Ants protect aphids from predators such as ladybugs.

Ants and Other Insects

Aphids are not the only insects that make honeydew; **scale insects**, tree-hoppers and leafhoppers all produce honeydew. They are attended and usually protected by ants. One kind of ant from Africa collects scale insects and takes them back to its nest inside the hollow stems of living plants. The scale insects live a protected life inside the stem, feeding on sap and making honeydew, which the ants eat. This is another kind of symbiosis.

The caterpillars of some butterflies, especially the blues, spend part of their lives as caterpillars in the nests

An ant feeds off a liquid produced by the imperial blue caterpillar.

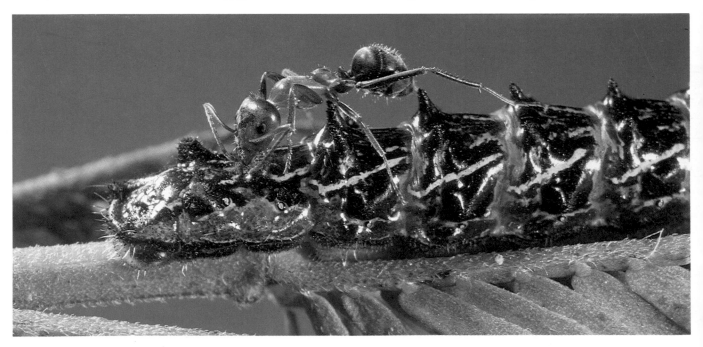

of ants. The caterpillars have tough, horny skins, which the ants cannot bite. They feed on the ants' larvae, but they also produce a sweet secretion, which the ants eat.

Many other types of caterpillars are killed and eaten by ants. Swallow-tail caterpillars, however, are well-protected. Behind the head they have a gland that is normally hidden, but if the caterpillar is bothered by ants, the gland sticks out and gives off a foul smell, which drives the ants away.

In most parts of the world, however, ants are the major enemies of other insects and they are very successful **predators**.

Ants feeding from scale insects.

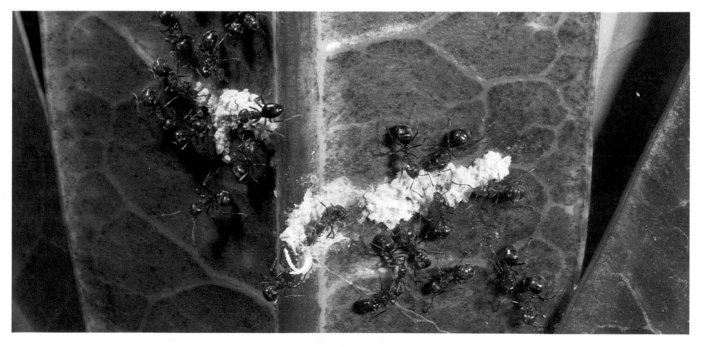

The Guests of Ants

Many kinds of small creatures live all, or part, of their lives in the nests of ants. They are usually called the "guests" of ants. Many guests give off special scents that either calm the ants down or trick them into treating the guest as another worker ant. Most guests are insects, but one of the commonest and easiest to find is not an insect. It is a tiny, white woodlouse (a crustacean). Under flat stones covering ant nests you may see them running around with the ants. The ants seem to take no notice of them. The woodlice live in the nests of many kinds of ants and they eat leftovers. They also eat the honeydew of root-feeding aphids, which the ants may have in the nest.

Many ant guests are scavengers, feeding on rubbish in the nest. The strange larvae of a kind of flowerfly do this. The larvae are so different from normal fly larvae that at first,

The histerid beetle (1 and 2) grooms adult ants and eats their larvae. The white woodlouse (3) lives only in ants' nests where it cleans up by eating scraps.

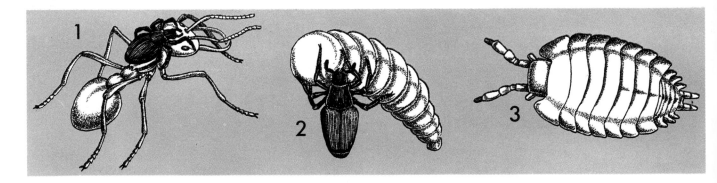

scientists thought they were some kind of slug or scale insect.

Some of the most interesting guests of ants are beetles. Some kinds are scavengers, others eat the eggs and larvae of the ants or even trick worker

Another ant "guest" is the flowerfly larva. It is a scavenger and eats any rubbish in the nest.

ants into feeding them liquid food from their mouths.

Ants and Plants

Many different kinds of animals, including insects, eat plants. The plants can defend themselves in various ways. Thorns keep away big grazing animals. Many plants store poisons in their leaves. And some plants have ants to guard and protect them.

In Central America, there are acacia trees that have hollow thorns. A particular kind of ant nests inside the

These ants protect their home and food source, an acacia tree.

Ants get nectar from wild ginger.

thorns. Apart from a place to nest, the acacia provides the ants with two kinds of food: nectar from the leaf stalks and oils and **proteins** from little growths on the leaves. The ants collect these growths and take them to the nest. In return for food and shelter, the ants, armed with powerful stings, chase away leaf-eating and sap-sucking insects.

A scientist studied the trees and their ants. He found that if he removed the ants from the trees, lots of insects moved in and the trees became sickly. So, the ants really do protect the trees. This is another good example of symbiosis.

In Africa there are other kinds of acacia trees that have ants nesting on them.

5
The Enemies of Ants

This is the position a wood ant takes up to threaten an enemy.

Defending the Nest

A large ant nest is attractive to a wide range of enemies. The eggs, larvae, pupae and even the adult ants themselves, are a rich food for any predator that can get at them.

Ants have many ways of defending themselves. Some kinds of ants have a group of workers with specially enlarged, toughened heads. Such a worker spends most of its time blocking the single nest entrance with its head. It moves aside only to let in returning workers, which it recognizes by their smell; each ant colony has its own smell, most of which comes from a pair of glands in the thorax of each worker. Nest-mates can therefore recognize each other by their smell. They attack strange ants because they do not have the correct smell.

Ants also have chemical weapons.

Some have nasty stings, which is not surprising because ants are related to wasps. Others squirt out formic acid from their tail ends. The acid burns and has a bad smell. Some ants use their powerful jaws as well as chemicals to deter enemies.

If a single ant is attacked, it can "call" for help by squirting out a special alarm scent that alerts other workers, which rush to its aid.

Ants defend their brood and nest against a pill bug.

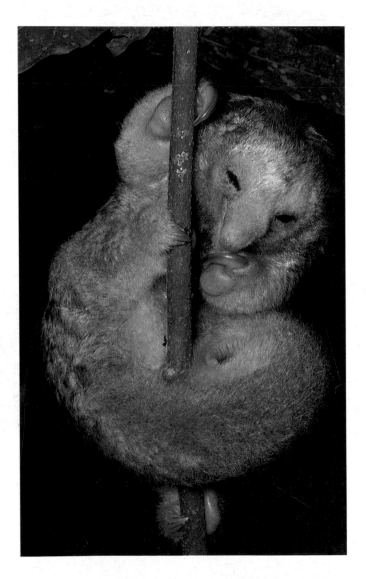

A silky anteater from Central America.

Anteaters and Birds

Many animals depend mainly or entirely on ants for food. In South America, the silky anteater eats ants that nest in trees and vines. It avoids those with big jaws like army ants and leaf-cutters. Like all true anteaters, it has no teeth. Instead, it has a very long tongue, which it can shoot out to lap up ants. The tongue is covered with sticky saliva, and the anteater has strong claws to break open the ant nests.

There are several kinds of birds, like woodpeckers, that like to eat ants. Others prefer ants to most other insects and, not surprisingly, are called ant birds. Not only do they eat ants but they also follow the trails of army ants and eat the insects flushed out by the marching columns.

Other birds have a use for ants but do not actually eat them. Instead, they wallow among ants, picking some up in their bills to crush them into their feathers, especially under the wings. This is called "anting" and it is thought that this is part of the birds' grooming behavior. Formic acid and other chemicals made by the ants can act as an **insecticide** and may reduce the numbers of lice and fleas in the feathers.

The green woodpecker likes to eat ants as well as other insects.

A jay grooms itself using ants. This is called "anting."

Termites and Other Ants

All over the world, there are many ants that eat **termites.** To protect themselves many kinds of termites have developed weapons. Some have jaws of unequal size. This enables the termite to flick ants away in an action rather like a human flicking finger

Slave-making ants steal larvae from the nest they have raided.

against thumb. Other termites squirt sticky poisons at ants.

Ants may themselves be the enemies of other ants. Some kinds specialize in raiding the nests of other ants to steal their larvae and pupae for food. Others, called slave-making ants, are fierce fighters and have large, curved jaws, but they cannot do household jobs in their own nests.

Every now and then, a raiding party of slave-making ants leaves the nest to look for a colony of another kind of ant. The slave-makers kill any workers that try to defend the colony

A soldier termite from Kenya guards its nest.

and then return to their own nest with the worker cocoons of their victims.

Soon the captured pupal cocoons hatch into workers, which live as slaves. They behave as they would in their own nest, gathering food for the slave-makers and cleaning and repairing the nest. The slave workers also look after the larvae of the slave-making ant. All of them live in the cooler parts of the world.

6
Ants as Pets

Yellow field ants and their pupae.

Making an Ant House

It is easy to keep a colony of ants as pets. A simple kind of ant house can be made out of a transparent plastic box, which you can buy in most hardware stores. Ask an adult to make some air holes in the lid with a hot needle. Inside your box you will need a smaller plastic box with a hole in one side. This will be used as a chamber for the ants, especially the queen. Ants do not like light shining into their nest, so cover the smaller box with red cellophane, which you can see through but the ants cannot.

Your ants will need food and water. Soak a small piece of sponge in water, or in a weak solution of honey and water, and place it inside the smaller box. A little piece of cake and some chopped worm can be put into the outer box for the ants to eat. Do not leave uneaten food to go moldy.

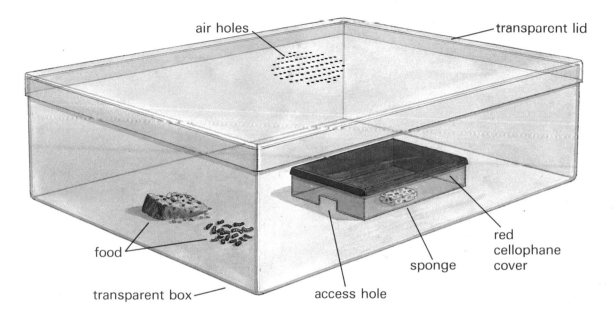

air holes   transparent lid

transparent box

food

access hole

sponge

red
cellophane
cover

All you need now are the ants. The best kind to look for is the small common garden ant. You can often find a colony under a stone. Collect them gently by pushing them into a narrow-necked bottle with a small, soft paintbrush. You can also collect eggs, larvae and pupae. Transfer them all to your plastic box and watch the workers sort things out.

If you cannot find a nest, look for newly-mated queens. In cold countries these are the fat, flying ants you see in summer; in tropical countries you may see ants on their mating flights at any time of the year. It is best to put several queens into your ant house together. This way you can watch the growth of a colony from the beginning. Remember that the queen will not feed until the first eggs have become workers.

Glossary

Abdomen   The rear part of an insect's body; it contains the stomach, sex organs, and in some insects the sting and poison glands.

Antennae   The two feelers on the head of an insect; the feelers are sensitive to touch and smell.

Aphids   Small insects, which suck the juices from plants.

Brood   A number of young animals produced at one hatching.

Colonies   Groups of the same type of animal or plant living or growing together.

Compost   A mixture of manure or rotting vegetable matter, for fertilizing soil.

Crop   A pouch in the abdomen in which food is stored.

Honeydew   The sweet liquid excreted by aphids and similar insects.

Insecticide   A chemical that kills insects.

Larva   The grub that hatches from an insect's egg.

Leaf litter   The dead leaves that carpet the forest floor.

Mating   The joining together of a male and a female animal so that the female's eggs are fertilized by the male's sperm.

Node   A knob, or swelling; in insects, a bump on the waist between thorax and abdomen.

Ovary   The gland in the abdomen of female animals which makes eggs.

Predators   Animals that hunt and kill other animals for food.

Prey   An animal that is killed and eaten by another animal.

Proteins   Substances that are vital to the growth and health of animals and plants.

Pupa   The stage in the growth of an insect when the larva is broken down and reformed into an adult.

Queen   The egg-laying female in an ant, bee or wasp colony.

Saliva   The liquid produced in the mouth from glands in the head.

Scale insects   Small insects that live and feed on plants and secrete a protective shell around themselves.

Scavengers   Animals that feed on dead animals.

Social   Living together in a colony.
Sperm   Male sex cells, which are used to fertilize a female's eggs.
Symbiosis   A close association of two different kinds of animals or plants that is often of benefit to each.
Termites   Social insects that live together in colonies. They are sometimes called white ants but they are not related to ants at all.
Testes   Glands in the abdomen of male animals; the testes make sperm.
Thorax   The middle part of the body of an insect. The thorax bears three pairs of legs and, in male and queen ants, also bears two pairs of wings.

Finding Out More

The following books will help you to find out more about ants.

Batten, Mary. *The Tropical Forest: Ants, Ants, Animals and Plants.* New York: Crowell Junior Books, 1973.

Cook, David. *The Small World of Ants.* New York: Franklin Watts, 1981.
Darling, Kathy. *Ants Have Pets.* Easton, MD: Garrard, 1977.
Lisker, Tom. *Terror in the Tropics: The Army Ants.* Milwaukee, MN: Raintree Publishers, 1977.
Overbeck, Cynthia. *Ants.* Minneapolis: Lerner Publications, 1982.

All photographs from Oxford Scientific Films by the following photographers: K. Atkinson 23; G.I. Bernard cover, 10, 19; J.A.L. Cooke frontispiece, 12, 17, 24, 26, 27, 30, 31, 33, 42; M. Fogden 38; Mantis Wildlife Films 22; S. Morris 41; P. O'Toole 18, 28, 37; D.J. Saunders 39; P.K. Sharpe 8, 14, (bottom), 25, 34; T. Shepherd 13; D. Thompson 29; G. Thompson 14 (top), 35; P. & W. Ward 20; B.E. Watts 9, 36. Artwork by Wendy Meadway.

Index